Ashton's Hope;

A Journey of Courage, Faith, and

Unconditional Love

Fawn Snyder

ISBN 13: 979-8653296260

This book is dedicated to my beautiful baby girl Ashton who grew up to become my best friend. I admire her for her huge heart, her unshakable faith and her ability to always cheer me up when I need it the most.

I also dedicate this book to my amazing family: my husband Jim, my son Gregory, my son Seth and my daughter-in-law Ann. We may not always see eye to eye, but we always have each other's back. I can't leave out my two beautiful grand-daughters Noel and Hope, who have blessed my life more than I could ever imagine.

One more group of people I'd like to dedicate this book to is everyone who battles mental illness daily. Your courage is admired.

Table of Contents

Introduction

Mental illness can be hard to understand, and even harder to accept when your child is diagnosed with it. For approximately ten years, my daughter Ashton and I searched for answers regarding her symptoms: tiredness, low energy, and no desire to engage in family activities. We were searching for a physical or medical diagnosis. Not until after Ashton's first suicide attempt was she given a proper diagnosis of Bipolar Disorder.

This book reflects on our journey together, how it affected our family, and how I as a mother struggled with my daughter's illness. I doubted my effectiveness as a parent and blamed myself for the hell that Ashton had to endure. I have a nursing degree and worked many years on a telemetry/medical floor, and that is the direction my mind was leading me while searching for answers. I studied mental health in nursing school but never thought that Ashton's issues where linked to a mental illness.

I learned that education on mental illness was very insightful, as is education on any subject. It was a subject that we were not familiar with.

My faith was tested, but also strengthened by this journey. At the time, I felt abandoned by God; but, now that I look back, I can see how He was with us all along

I wrote this book to encourage and help others dealing with a mental illness, but also because of my own need to write it, and found the writing therapeutic for myself. I have written this book using fictitious names at the request of Ashton. We live in a very small community and I wanted to respect her privacy.

Overview

I've heard somewhere along the line that love has no boundaries. I totally agree with this statement. But I believe—and have learned first-hand—that depression also has no boundaries. This disease can afflict anyone no matter their gender, race, religion, monetary status, or age. Depression is a disease that is so difficult to comprehend—as most mental illnesses are. It is not a disease that can be physically seen. When I was growing up in the '70s, depression didn't seem so prevalent, or maybe it just wasn't talked about. Still to this day mental illness carries a certain stigma. People are willing to talk about their blood pressure, their diabetes, or even their bowel movements, but not so quick to reveal that they suffer from a mental illness. It seems to be an embarrassment or a sign of weakness. I sometimes wonder if the stressors of our fast-paced world play a role, especially with depression. Most of the time I feel as if I can't keep up with all the tasks I need to accomplish from day to day. (Who else needs to write all their logins and passwords in a little book like myself?)

When I was younger, life was so much simpler. We did not have all the electronics and social media that is available at our fingertips today. People seemed kinder, genuine, and more neighborly. In this age there seems to be so much pressure on image and what can be attained monetarily, and that determines a person's success. I feel people with mental illness don't willingly reveal their illness due to the fear of rejection or judgment from the rest of the world.

Mental illness: I have lived and learned about this horrible disease through my best friend, who also happens to be my daughter Ashton. She has suffered over half of her life from this debilitating disorder. I have witnessed her courage, her determination, and her faith in our Lord Jesus Christ as it brought her through extremely difficult times. I suffered right alongside her. When you are a mother that would give your child your last breath, you hurt when they hurt. This disease has also affected our entire family. I would like to share Ashton's journey, as well as mine as a mother of a child battling mental illness. Although I am not a medical expert on this topic, I have learned a lot about it along the way.

I hope to help others afflicted with mental illnesses by sharing our experiences, and bring hope to those who are struggling along this path—perhaps strange and frightening for them, but familiar to me.

CHAPTER ONE

What is Depression?

There are several types of mental illnesses, but I am focusing mainly on depression because this is the illness with which Ashton's journey began. According to the American Psychiatric Association: "Depression (major depressive disorder) is a common and serious medical condition that negatively affects how you feel, the way you think and how you act. Fortunately, it is also treatable. Depression causes feelings of sadness and or loss of interest in activities once enjoyed. It can lead to a variety of emotions and physical problems and can decrease a person's ability to function at work or home."[1]

---

[1] psychiatry.org

Mayo Clinic states, "Although depression may occur only once during your life, people typically have multiple episodes. During these episodes, symptoms occur most of the day nearly every day and may include: *Feelings of sadness, tearfulness, emptiness or hopelessness. *Angry outbursts, irritability or frustration even over small matters. *Loss of interest or pleasure in most or all normal activities such as sex, hobbies or sports. *Sleep disturbances including insomnia or sleeping too much. *Tiredness and lack of energy, so even small tasks take extra effort. *Reduced appetite and weight loss or increased cravings for food and weight gain. *Anxiety, agitation and restlessness. *Slowed thinking, speaking or body movements. *Feelings of worthlessness or guilt, fixation on the past failures or self-blame. *Trouble thinking, concentrating, making decisions and remembering things. *Frequent or recurrent thoughts of death, suicidal thoughts, suicide attempts or suicide. *Unexplained physical problems such as back pain or headaches.[2]" The Mayo Clinic also describes depression as more than just a bout of the blues. Depression isn't a weakness. You

---

[2] mayoclinic.org

can't simply snap out of it, and may actually require long-term treatment. Most people feel better with medication, psychotherapy, or both. Common signs and symptoms of depression in children, teenagers, and older adults are similar but there are some differences.

As per re:MIND (formerly dbsahouston): "There are many names for the different types of depression. Depression often co-exists with other mental or physical illnesses. Substance abuse, anxiety disorders and eating disorders are particularly common conditions that may be worsened by depression and it is important that depression and each co-occurring illness be appropriately diagnosed and treated. Substance use disorders (abuse and dependence) also frequently co-occur with depression.[3]"

Quoted from Harvard Health Publications from Harvard Medical School: "It is often said that depression results from chemical imbalance, but that figure of speech doesn't capture how complex the disease is. Research suggests that depression doesn't spring from simply having too much or too little of certain brain chemicals. Rather, there are many possible causes of

---

[3] remindsupport.org

depression including faulty mood regulation by the brain, genetic vulnerability, stressful life events, medications and medical problems. It's believed that several of these forces interact to bring on depression. Neurotransmitters are chemicals that relay messages from neuron to neuron. An anti-depressant medication tends to increase the concentration of these substances in the spaces between the neurons (the synapses). In many cases, this shift appears to give the system enough of a nudge so that the brain can do its job better. With the level of complexity, you can see how two people might have similar symptoms of depression, but the problem on the inside, and therefore what treatments will work best may be entirely different[4]."

I could go on and on with research quotes, but there is a vast amount of information available to anyone who is interested. I believe the information I quoted gives a general idea of what defines depression, and a lot of this helps me to understand my daughter's past behaviors and choices. I myself suffer from seasonal depression along with what I call event depression. Seasonal depression for me is the oncoming of fall. I

---

[4] health.harvard.edu

consider fall "pre-death" because to me winter is death. I am not fond of winter to say the least. I never was and probably never will be. Winter in my mind brings the cold, the gray skies, the loss of living plants and greenery, and the confinement to the four walls of my home. I try to schedule activities to get myself out of the house and enjoy the beautiful world we live in. Usually the cold deters me. The loss of my brother is what I consider event or situational depression. I hold onto the good memories, and hopefully time will help me deal with this loss. Event depression can occur with any loss or significant change in your life that is upsetting to your well-being. When my daughter experiences her darkest moments, I do as well. Nothing in the world seems right until she is better. It's like a dark cloud that hangs over me until she is well. I consider this another example of event depression.

But my depression is nothing compared to what my daughter has endured, and as her mom I wish I could take this dreaded disease from her.

CHAPTER TWO

———————————

Our Family History

Jim and I met when we were in our teens at a church Halloween party. We both finished high school and got married. Neither of us attended college and therefore joined the workforce. Jim worked construction and I was a waitress. We struggled financially. Sometimes we managed to make ends meet and sometimes we didn't, but we persevered. We originally wanted to have six kids, the big house with the white picket fence, and for me to be a stay-at-home mom.

I've learned over the years that life doesn't always turn out the way you planned: it turns out the way God has planned.

We had our fair share of struggles but managed to stay together "for better or for worse." We waited five years before starting our family. Gregory was born in 1983, Ashton in 1985, and Seth in 1986. We wasted no time once we got started. Our children became our lives.

Jim's construction business was very slow, so we moved out of state to the sunny south for better job opportunities. Our children were one, two, and four years of age at that time. I got another waitress job while Jim continued in the construction field. We lived in a one room efficiency motel for four months in order to save enough money to rent a house. We did not have a lot, but it was easier to make those ends meet. We did a lot of free and inexpensive things with the kids for entertainment: we went to the beach a lot; fishing was one of Gregory's all-time favorite things to do; and the local movie theater offered free movies on Saturday afternoon for the kids. Story time at the library was also a freebie. We got involved in a wonderful Baptist Church, which always had activities going on. Jim coached both of our boys in Little League baseball and football. My children had a great childhood. Like I said earlier we did not have much money, but we lived for our kids. Those were much simpler times that I would gladly return to in a heartbeat.

When Gregory started school, I entered nursing school at a local community college. I never planned on becoming a nurse, but that was another intervention from God. When I graduated from nursing school, I was missing my family up north. We made the decision to move back home—not to the city from which we came, but to a little country town about an hour away. We rented a house on 35 acres with a pond and a big old barn. Although this was not my dream, it was my husband's. I was a city girl with no desire to live on a farm, but it got me closer to home and, I must admit, it was beautiful.

After renting this place for three months the owner wanted to sell it and we were blessed to purchase our first home. That story was another one of God's divine interventions. I look back now and see how God had led us on this path he had chosen for us. No doubt about it! He was placing us right where he wanted us. For some time, I desired to move back to the sunny south but now I realize we are where we are meant to be. Jim continued in the construction field and I took my first nursing job. Our kids were now in elementary school. As they started a new school, we all started a new chapter in our lives.

CHAPTER THREE

Ashton's History

Ash was a quiet, kind, sweet, happy child. She was very shy in social situations, but always polite and well mannered. Even as a middle child with an older brother and a younger brother, she was always the peace maker. Not a mean bone in her body, and she remains the same to this day. She was always loving, and exceptionally kind. I felt a little guilt for moving my children away from their friends, school, and familiar surroundings, but believed that they were young and would adjust. Ash was in fourth grade at the time of the move, and I know it affected her the most. She was shy to begin with and struggled for a while, but eventually made friends. She had a few good friends throughout junior and senior high. I believe she played one year on the tennis team in junior high. Her grades were average, and she sought help when needed.

She and I had, and still have, an incredible relationship. She is truly my best friend. We always loved to shop, and of course "do lunch." Shopping for school clothes and prom dresses were always good times for us. I did not notice any difference in her behavior until around the age of sixteen.

A lot of our shopping trips ended with her sleeping on the way home as I drove. I just figured she was tired. I loved her company, so I didn't mind if she slept. With her sixteenth birthday approaching, I asked her what she wanted for her special day. All she wanted was for her and I to spend a couple of days together at the beach. I worked a few extra shifts and we took our trip. We shopped, laid on the beach and of course ate out. I felt honored that she just wanted time with me instead of gifts. My husband and I consider our children as our biggest blessings from God and we truly cherish and appreciate them. We have always given them our time and unconditional love. To me, being a mom is the best job imaginable.

Then, around that same time, I noticed some changes in her behavior. She was sleeping a lot more, worrying about her looks, worrying about her weight, and not hanging with her friends as much. I rationalized these things to some degree. Worrying about her looks and weight seemed normal to me for this age. Sleeping more really didn't concern me either; I figured she was getting up early for school and staying up late to study. And I thought that maybe her interests were changing, which was why she was not hanging with her friends. She got into running and took what seemed to be forever to do her make up before leaving the house. When I questioned her about always being in bed, her reply was that she was just so tired. As a nurse, I tried to diagnose her, as most of us medical people do. I thought she could have a thyroid issue, anemia, lupus, etc. I took her to our family doctor who, after talking with Ashton, diagnosed her with depression and put her on an anti-depressant.

Things did not improve. She was still sleeping a lot and had little motivation to participate in family activities or life itself. I took her back to the doctors and inquired about getting some blood work completed to test for anemia, thyroid, lupus—something to explain why she was always tired. The doctor ordered the blood work she felt was appropriate and the results all came back within normal limits. Ashton continued to sleep a lot and became even more isolative. I thought maybe it was just normal teenage stuff—hormones, or her wanting her space—so I let her stay in her room and sleep. I would try to encourage her to join us for family outings, but her reply was usually that she was too tired. She completed her homework, went running, and did all the things that were required of her, but still seemed to sleep more than normal.

As a nurse, I felt that I should have noticed that these were signs of depression. I beat myself up for a long time for not realizing this. It did not cross my mind. I know Ash was on anti-depressants in the past, but they did not seem to help, so I dismissed the idea and was searching for a medical reason for her symptoms. Maybe I did not believe that my daughter could have depression. It did not run in our family to my knowledge. What would she have to be depressed about anyway? She was beautiful, had a good home life, and was very loved. I just wasn't educated enough to realize that these things don't protect someone from depression.

At the age of seventeen, Ashton came to me one summer afternoon out on the deck and said, "I have to tell you something and I don't want to upset you." I said "OK." She removed a towel from her forearm and showed me a bleeding cut on the inside of her arm. She was concerned that we might have to go to the ER for stitches. Half panicking, I asked what had happened and she explained that she was cutting herself. I didn't comprehend. Why on Earth would anyone want to do this to themselves on purpose? She explained about "cutting" and stated that she thought she had gone too deep this time.

"'This time?'" I asked. "What do you mean 'this time?'"

Ash explained that for her, cutting was a release that helped her to feel pain. I did not understand this at all. How stupid did I feel that I never noticed that she always wore long sleeves, even in the summer? We talked and she confided in me that she was also struggling with bulimia. I knew that she ran and exercised a lot, but bulimia? How could she think that she was fat? She weighed a little over one hundred pounds.

How could I, as her best friend, her Mom, and a nurse be so blind to all of this going on with her? The fact is, Ash was ashamed to tell me, and was so good at hiding it all. How could my sweet daughter be so depressed that she would do this to herself? The guilt set in. What did I do wrong? Did I not tell her how beautiful she was? Did I not hug her enough? Did I not tell her how much she was loved? I felt like such a failure as a mother. My beautiful daughter was suffering right before my eyes and I did not see it. I just wanted to fix her. What pain was she talking about? She was young, beautiful inside and out, and had her whole life ahead of her. What did she have to be depressed about? Was I so wrapped up in my own life that I didn't see all of this? I had a full-time job, was trying to help my husband build a Christmas tree farm business, take care of a house, attend my children's school functions. You know, normal everyday stuff; but perhaps my child's well-being should have been my main concern. I blamed myself. How could I not? I felt that I had failed at the most important job in my life.

CHAPTER FOUR

After High School

Ashton graduated high school and had not chosen a career path. She was undecided on what her calling exactly was, and went straight into the work force. She worked local jobs around town. She was very good at all of them, and was a good employee. She appeared to be leading a normal life but just couldn't decide on a career choice. She continued taking her anti-depressant medication and attended outpatient therapy intermittently as she felt she needed. She would go on family vacations and seemed to enjoy herself. She still was isolative at times and continued to "sleep her life away" as I put it. We remained close but I felt that she truly wasn't happy. She knew how to put on a good front.

There were times when she was okay. We talked almost daily unless our work schedules didn't allow it. I tried to keep her busy with activities around the house to keep her out of her room. I would try to spend my days off with her as well. I encouraged her to find hobbies to occupy her time. She couldn't find anything that interested her except her exercising, which I think had become an addiction. It helped her feel in control of something, her weight. I found out years later that she wasn't always compliant with her medication. She didn't think she needed it and wanted to be "normal" like others her age without medication. She struggled from time to time with her bulimia and cutting but hid it from me. I tried not to pry too much into her adult life but wanted to keep an eye on her. If I asked about these issues, she would offer some information at times, and at other times would be evasive.

When Ashton turned twenty-one, her love of alcohol scared the crap out of me. I knew she was drinking before then, but now the bar scene was very appealing to her. She became a little isolative with me. She always worked full-time and payed her bills. Her personality hadn't changed, and she was still the sweetest person imaginable. Some nights she came home very late and I knew she was at the bar. I knew she was of age, but a mother never stops worrying. Most times if I called her cell phone, she would answer, which eased by mind. But I had a lot of sleepless nights when she would not answer her phone. I worried about her drinking and driving, but always told her to call for a ride if she needed one. I love my daughter unconditionally and my biggest fear is losing one of my children. Alcohol seems to go hand-in-hand with depression, at least for Ashton. Maybe it helped her numb her pain. Alcoholism is prevalent in our family history as we have lost several family members to this disease. She also used alcohol as a crutch before social functions to help her cope with her social anxiety.

CHAPTER FIVE

Ashton's Other Disorders

Ashton also suffered from other disorders that are common with depression. She dealt with social anxiety, OCD (Obsessive Compulsive Disorder), and body dysmorphic disorder. I'm not sure when these disorders came about, but likely during her teenage years. Regarding her social anxiety disorder, when we would go to a restaurant we would have to request to be seated in the most isolated section. Speaking to family at reunions was very uncomfortable for her, and like I mentioned earlier, alcohol would help her cope with these situations. Ashton also became overwhelmed with crowds, triggering panic attacks for which she was prescribed Xanax. This seemed to help at times.

I believe her weight became an obsession. As mentioned before, I believe Ash felt her weight was something she had control over, unlike her depression. I asked her how her bulimia began. She told me when she was in high school, she would notice other girls throwing up their lunches in the bathroom. These girls were thin and popular. She figured this was something she could do to control her weight. She started counting every calorie and would partake in excessive exercise to burn a certain number of calories. But then she would binge-eat, and felt the need to purge.

Her OCD was always out of control. It extended into what some might view as very odd behaviors. She was always late for everything, which was attributed to her OCD. She would have to check electrical outlets several times before leaving the house. She had to unplug her hair dryer, the toaster, lamps, etc. and would have to hold the unplugged cord in her hand and count to a certain number or she believed something bad was going to happen. She also had to pump the liquid hand soap dispenser a certain number of times as well.

Regarding her body dysmorphic disorder, I did not understand this at all. My daughter is drop-dead gorgeous, but felt that she was so unattractive. She did not see what the rest of the world saw. Guys always gave her a second look. She had many guys interested in dating her. Her expectation of herself was perfection by the world's standards. She would spend an enormous amount of time doing her make up. If it wasn't perfect the first time, off it would come, and she would start all over again. I blame her disease for this, but also the society in which we live that promotes perfection. Ashton's perception of her appearance was one of the reasons for her first suicide attempt: she felt she wasn't pretty enough, thin enough, or good enough for any-one.

CHAPTER SIX

She Tried to Cope

Ash always tried to improve herself and fit into this world. She tried different jobs, tried to go out of her comfort zone by socializing to fit in, and always seemed to be searching for her career path. In her dating life, she seemed attracted to guys that weren't right for her. She had low self-esteem, and guys took advantage of that, emotionally and physically. I longed for her to find someone who would appreciate her for the beautiful soul that she was. Someone to cherish her as I did and to love her unconditionally. I believe she stayed in most of her relationships because she just wanted to be with someone, or because she thought she deserved to be treated the way they treated her.

In 2012 at the age of twenty-seven, she decided to start nursing school with her sister-in-law Ann. Ann and Ashton were the same age and had become good friends. Ash did well her first couple of semesters of school. We thought she had found her calling. But then she started to struggle in the third semester and dropped out. It wasn't just the school work that she was struggling with at that time; she became consumed by her appearance to the point of getting Botox to improve on a particular facial feature that she was obsessed with. She was convinced that no one at her age had this issue and that no one would be interested in dating her because of it. This feature was unnoticeable to everyone but her. To her, this flaw was devastating. In addition to receiving Botox, she also researched plastic surgeons and had made an appointment for a consultation. She invited me to go to one of these consultations with her to inquire about a face lift. I reluctantly went in hopes that the doctor would tell her he saw no need for surgery. He did indeed tell her just that and I was relieved. I thought that would be the end of it. Ash thought that I had called the doctor ahead of time and told him what to say. Delusional thinking right there. At that point I did not know enough about her disease or mental illnesses to recognize that's what it was. If I was educated more back then, I might have been able to guide her and maybe help her combat this way of thinking.

CHAPTER SEVEN

Her First Suicide Attempt

Ashton was so obsessed with this delusional distortion of her face that in the fall of 2013, at the age of twenty-eight, she made the decision to end her life.

Just typing these words sends shivers down my spine and brings back a flood of emotions. She felt as though she was a burden to us and that we would all be better off without her. One day while we were all at work, Ash went into her brother's home and got his hunting rifle and shells. She had no idea how to load a gun but was determined to figure it out. She walked back into our woods with a plan of propping the gun up aimed at her head with a string around the trigger. She decided to fire the gun first to ensure that her plan would work. The gun was so loud that it scared her and hurt her ears, and she abandoned her plan. God was protecting her that day. Thank you Lord for your mercy.

Ash's ears continued to ring after firing the gun. She went to an ear, nose and throat specialist for help. She did not tell them that she had planned to commit suicide. They told her it could take a while for the ringing to subside.

She did not tell me about her attempt until three days later. Her ears continued to ring so she came to me for advice. I was freaking out inside and felt as though I wanted to vomit. A suicide attempt? How did it get to this point? Thank God she did not succeed. I knew she was obsessed with her looks, but suicide? I told her dad and we watched her constantly. We didn't know what else to do. A few days later, she went into the barn to talk to her dad. She stated that her ears were still ringing, and she could not take it anymore. She asked him if there were any legal way to kill herself. At that point we knew we had to act. We called our local emergency room and they referred us to psychiatric hospital about an hour away. Jim and I drove Ashton there and sat in the psychiatric emergency room for seven hours until she could be evaluated. She was committed and we rode home in silence except for my crying all the way home.

Ash had quit taking her medications prior to nursing school because she didn't think she needed them. I believe that was the beginning of her downward spiral into psychosis. She was not properly diagnosed and was not on the correct medications.

Ash remained in the psychiatric hospital for about a week. She was diagnosed with depression and discharged on new medications with instructions to follow up with a therapist in two to three days. We could not get a therapy appointment for ten days. She remained suicidal due to the continued ringing in her ears and had to be watched constantly. I had to take a leave of absence from work to protect her. I slept with her, followed her to the bathroom, removed all razors from the shower, hid all medications in the house and made sure she took her prescribed medications.

Jim and I would have very long daily conversations with her, trying to reason with her. We tried to reassure her that her ears would stop ringing and she would be fine. Nothing mattered or got through to her. She was still contemplating suicide. She was only out of the hospital a week and we had to commit her again.

The night we had to commit her again was a nightmare for our family. It was one night I don't want to ever experience again. To this day, thinking about it makes me cry. During one of the nightly conversations between Ash, Jim, and I, Ash started screaming that we should just let her die. Jim and I had barricaded her in her bedroom and tried to calm her down. She climbed out the window and was going to jump off the roof. I had to climb out on the roof after her and literally throw her back inside. I told Jim to keep her in her room and I was going to call some places to find out where we should take her. While I was on the phone, Jim yelled "She got away from me!" It was dark out and Ashton took off through the Christmas tree fields towards the pond. Jim went after her and I went to our son Greg's house next door to get him, Seth, and Ann for help. They all took off towards the pond and I ran to get a flashlight. On my way back to the fields I saw a sight that is etched in my mind forever. I saw Greg with tears streaming down his face, carrying his sister over his shoulder. She was kicking and screaming "Just let me die!"

Gregory said to me, "I got her, you better go check on dad. He's on the ground at the bottom of the hill. I'm not sure if he's having a heart attack or what."

I ran to check on Jim as Greg, Seth, and Ann stayed with Ashton to ensure her safety. When I got to Jim, he was still on the ground having a difficult time breathing and sobbing. He kept saying "I just couldn't keep up with her." We were all devastated. Jim and I made the trip back to our local emergency room. They recommended that we take Ashton back to the psychiatric hospital where she was previously—an hour away. As Jim drove, I sat in the back seat with Ash to keep her from jumping out of the car.

Upon arrival to the psychiatric hospital, we were informed that they had no available beds. They recommended for Jim and I to go home since it was late and a bed search could take a while. We left our sweet daughter in their care with some relief knowing that she was safe for now. An available bed was found overnight and she was transferred to their care. I was losing hope that we would ever find answers and stability for Ashton.

Ashton was in that facility for almost another week. She was started on all different medications and discharged with instructions to follow up with a therapist in two to three days as before. Again, we could not obtain an appointment for a week. We kept a close eye on her every minute, day and night. She tried to put on a good front but still complained of her ears ringing all the time. She still had suicidal thoughts, saying she could not live with the ringing.

It was Thanksgiving and Ash had been home for about a week. We had some family over for dinner and Ash was drinking to cope with the whole social situation. After our guests left, I went upstairs to check on her because I knew she drank a little too much. I found her passed out on our bed, blood on the sheets and a razor blade near her cut wrists. Her wrists were not cut in the manner of a suicide attempt but as she had cut in the past to release her pain. Jim and I loaded her into the car and headed back to our local emergency room once again.

CHAPTER EIGHT

Long Term Commitment

Ashton's alcohol level was too high for her to sign herself into the behavioral health unit on her own. She had to "sleep it off" overnight in the emergency room. Jim went home and I sat there alone by my daughter's side, crying and beating myself up as she slept. I thought I could have done something to prevent this. I felt like such a failure as a mom. The same old questions came rushing back into my mind. "Did I not tell her how beautiful she was?" "Did I not hug her enough as a child?" "Did I not tell her how much I loved her?" I sat there and sobbed, blaming myself for the suffering my daughter had to endure.

An angel then walked into the room. Her name was Tammy. She was Ashton's nurse for the night. I

knew her because this was the hospital where I
worked. Tammy took me into a private room, sat me
down, and told me to listen to her. She knew I was
blaming myself and told me that none of this was my
fault. She stated, "You are a wonderful mom and Ashton's condition was from nothing you did or didn't
do." She explained to me that this was a disease that
could be managed. She was so comforting. God placed
this angel right in front of me when I needed her. I will
never forget that intervention.

The next morning, Ashton's alcohol level was low
enough for admission to the behavioral health unit. She
was started on new medications and encouraged to
participate in group activities and meetings. Ash tried
but was not very successful opening up to others. That
social anxiety thing was still there.

She took her medications, but her main complaint
was the constant ringing in her ears. It had never quit
from when she fired that gun over two months ago.
She could not deal with it.

She was not making much improvement and the
decision was made to commit her to LTSR (Long Term
Structured Rehabilitation). She was not stable enough
to come home, and with her recent failed psychiatric

admissions, the psychiatrists felt this was the best option for her to stabilize and stay safe.

We did not know anything about LTSR and thought that Ash would be in and out in no time. I'm sure everything was explained to me, but at that point in my life, I truly was in shock from the whirlwind of events. I was so desperate for someone to "fix" Ashton and probably not comprehending like I should have. I probably thought there was an easy fix or a magic pill. I did not yet realize all the components needed to manage a mental illness.

Ash was transferred to LTSR within a few days. In the meantime, our family Christmas tree business had opened for the season. Needless to say, I certainly was not in my right mind to be happy and spread cheer. I just wanted to crawl in a hole and be left alone. I missed my daughter. Our family did our best to put on our happy faces to serve our customers and make their holiday season joyful while our world felt like it was falling apart. One of us was missing and we could all feel that void. We weren't whole but we did our best not to show that our hearts were broken. I remember so vividly standing in our gift shop pouring hot chocolate and just "losing it." My co-worker told me to take a

break and try to get it together. I did but it was short
lived. I would see moms with their daughters come
into the shop smiling and laughing. I would wonder to
myself "Am I ever going to have that with my daughter again? Is she ever going to be in her right mind
again?" Everyone was so happy and enjoying the season as they should be, but I was at one of my lowest
points in my life. How was I supposed to keep my
Christmas spirit going while my precious daughter
was away from us still wishing to die? She was supposed to be by my side serving hot chocolate and cook-
ies to our customers as we did every year. It was the
roughest tree season ever for me.

I drove to the LTSR home four to five nights per
week, sometimes with Jim but mostly alone. Jim and
the boys did not understand her mental illness or my
need to be by her side. They thought she should just
"snap out of it." Everyone tried to tell her to be thank-
ful for what she did have or that there were people in
this world that had worse problems. But when someone suffers from a mental illness, this kind of reasoning
is incomprehensible to them.

I was only allowed to visit Ash for 2 hours per
night. I wanted to be there seven nights a week, but

that was impossible with the Christmas tree business in full swing and the drive was an hour each way with the winter roads. I longed to hold her and comfort her. I thought I could make everything better and that no one knew my daughter better than I.

But I needed to step back and let the professionals help. Our visits were devastating to me. I was seeing no improvements in her condition after a few weeks. I only saw her getting worse.

Ashton was cooperative at times but still suicidal. She tried different methods to end her life. She would eat very little and had reverted back to making herself throw up her meals. She was losing weight rapidly. She was under one hundred pounds. Her clothes were falling off her to the point that I had to buy her smaller ones. She was gray in color, weak, and had bags under her eyes. She did not look like herself at all. When Jim would come with me to visit her, she would have him hold her. She would just sit on his lap, rock back and forth and just cry. She felt hopeless as we all did. The ringing in her ears was still her driving force to commit suicide. She tried to hoard pills to save them up in order to overdose. She took a drinking glass from the kitchen back to her room, broke it and stated to cut her arms again. After that incident, the staff moved her into a bedroom closer to the nurse's station for closer monitoring. She also left tampons in trying to get toxic shock syndrome. She was so desperate to kill herself due to the ringing in her ears. She could not tolerate it any longer. It had been 4 months at this point.

During our visits we would pray that God would take the ringing away. I would buy her inspirational books and send her cards three to four times per week. We would talk about all the good times we had shared, and I would encourage her to make plans of things she wanted to do with me when she got home. This was all just a temporary distraction for her. She could not think about the future. In her mind, there was no future. Ash spent a lot of time reading her Bible and praying. She also spent her allotted computer time emailing pastors and churches regarding healing services.

Ash finally became stable enough to get weekend home passes after 5 months of treatment. Her ears were still ringing all the time, but she wasn't suicidal.

At least that is what she was telling them in order to get a home pass. She had an ulterior motive. When she was home on a pass, we had to monitor and administer her medications. She was not allowed to go out alone or drive. Her first weekend home, she asked her brother Seth to take her to a healing service at one of the churches she had been in contact with. The pastor knew she was coming that particular weekend. He had her come up front during the service so he and other church members could pray over her for restoration of her hearing. Ash was disappointed when the ringing did not cease immediately and went back to LTSR at the end of her weekend visit with us. Over the course of the following week, the ringing in her ears lessened and by that Friday, was completely gone. The LTSR psychiatrist was skeptical when Ashton had told her of what had happened. Ash improved and after two weeks of being stable, was cleared for discharge.

Discharge day came after six long months and I thought to myself, "Hallelujah, the worst is behind us. We made it!" I had my best friend back, and all was once again right in my world.

Ashton had to follow up with a psychiatrist, go to therapy, and continue her medications. The psychiatrist at LTSR had diagnosed Ash with bipolar disorder and found a regimen of medications that seemed to work best for her. After a long ten years, we finally had a diagnosis, and some insight into her behaviors.

CHAPTER NINE

Back to Reality

Ash quickly got back into the dating scene and full-time employment. She seemed to be doing great. I believe she still had low self-esteem because in my mind, it showed in the type of guys she chose to date.

The first guy she dated post-LTSR was an old high school friend who was "Mr. Wonderful" for a few months. But soon, his true colors came out. He was possessive with a violent temper and abusive personality. Of course, alcohol played a huge role in a lot of his behaviors. Ash always enjoyed alcohol and old habits die hard. She was educated during her stay at LTSR that bipolar is a disease that can be managed through medication compliance, therapy, a regular sleep/wake cycle, and limited alcohol.

Ashton drank more than she should with her boyfriend and was not completely medication-compliant. She admitted to me that she missed some doses here and there. She also told me that she was angry over having this disease and that she felt it unfair. She did not ask for this. We always talked and I tried to keep her on track, but she became irritated with me at times. I'm sure I sometimes came across as lecturing, but I was concerned for her and her mental health. Being a Mom is the most important job in my life. I always want to protect my children, and I'm sure my concern occasionally comes across as nagging. Ash was young and wanted to enjoy her life without limitations. I believe she was fighting against her disease, or perhaps trying to prove to herself that she did not have it. I'm sure at times she thought she could live a "normal" life without medications.

Her abusive relationship came to an end and I was relieved. It was long overdue. Amen! She began dating again. She went back to the guy she was dating before her suicide attempt. They continued a rocky relationship for the next two years and then became engaged. Throughout those two years, I would frequently remind her to not become pregnant, as her LTSR psychiatrist recommended against it. If she did, she would have to go off her medications because they would be dangerous to the baby.

I saw red flags going off everywhere. It seemed as though she was withdrawing from us. She continued to abuse alcohol and was again not completely compliant with her medications. She confessed to me that she was not happy and still struggling with depression. She usually came to me for advice but seldom followed it.

About two weeks after her engagement, I noticed her spending a lot more time in bed. When I would ask her what was going on, thinking it was her depression, her reply was she was just tired. I finally figured it out. She was pregnant. I confronted her and she confirmed my suspicions.

To say the least, I was not happy. I was afraid for the baby's health due to Ash being on her medications. I was also afraid for my daughter as well, knowing that she would have to go off her medications completely. That scared the hell out of me. I should have been happy. I had no right feeling that way. I was going to be blessed with another grandchild.

Looking back now, I should have just trusted God. I should have accepted that he had a plan for Ashton's life. I feel God was testing my faith at that time in my life and I failed miserably. Little did I know at that time the journey we were all to embark on.

CHAPTER TEN

Round Two

I was going to be a grandma, or "Mawmaw" as my first sweet granddaughter Noel calls me. I felt so guilty because I was not excited like I was the first time. Inside, I was mad at Ashton for letting this happen. I tried to be supportive, but deep down I was just mad. How ashamed I am now of those feelings I had back then. Raising a child with her boyfriend was going to be rough financially and emotionally. I knew he wasn't the man God had made for her. He emotionally abused her and made her feel stupid and unworthy. She knew the relationship wasn't right for some time but had to get up the courage to end it. Being pregnant by him also made it a difficult and complicated choice—but she finally ended it. Her boyfriend did not take the break-up well and things got extremely ugly.

Ash seemed somewhat less stressed after things settled. She tried to carry on with her life the best she could. She had taken herself off all her medications "cold turkey" the moment she found out she was pregnant. She continued working full time, even with severe morning sickness. I was a nervous wreck because I knew what was coming, or I thought I did. Ash held it together for the most part and I thought "Okay, she can do this." On the other hand, I knew her bipolar disorder could not go untreated without some consequence. Soon enough the walls came crashing down.

I tried to support her daily. She had no one else. No boyfriend, and no close friends, so I was it. I tried to lift her up and encourage her the best I knew how, but like I said, bipolar cannot go untreated. Ash started to experience deeper depression, and panic attacks, and started to verbalize that she didn't know how much longer she could do this. I decided to give her a small baby shower with only eight close family members, thinking it would brighten her spirits. The day of the shower, I found her on the bathroom floor experiencing a total meltdown. She was crying and saying she couldn't go on. I took her to the emergency room, and she was discharged within a few hours. They could not put her on any psychiatric medications due to her pregnancy. We returned home and she tried to put on happy face for our guests who had waited for our return. Everyone was so supportive, and Ash made it through the day.

Ashton continued to struggle through each day. One day shortly after the baby shower, I passed where she worked, and her car was not there. When I got home, she was not there either. I called her to see if she was okay. She was at the emergency room alone. She had quit her job and took herself to the emergency room for admission. I rushed there in a panic. I sat with her until placement could be found in an accepting psychiatric facility. It was tough due to her being seven months pregnant. They had to worry about her safety with the possibility of being exposed to potentially violent patients. An accepting treatment facility was found that was two hours away and she was transported around 1:00am.

I was still working Monday through Friday but found myself making the two-hour trip three to four nights a week to visit Ashton. Sometimes Jim would come with me. I could not stay away. That was where my heart was at that moment in my life. The psychiatrist there started Ash on a low dose of an anti-depressant medication. We were assured that it was safe for pregnancy. Ash seemed to get worse. She became very suicidal and had to be put in the seclusion room due to her uncontrollable behavior. She would scream out and disrupt the unit. I believe this happened more than one time. When she wasn't in seclusion, she would refuse to come out of her room to participate in their programs. Jim and I would attend meetings with Ash and her psychiatrist to evaluate her progress and her plan of care. At one of these meetings, Ashton announced that she was giving the baby up for adoption, something she had never mentioned before. Jim and I were in shock. We told her that we would help her raise the baby, but her mind was made up.

She now was fixated on the perception that she was intellectually challenged and could not raise a child. She became so obsessed with her IQ that she requested an IQ test and was actually given one. Naturally she scored below average. She was out of her mind and psychotic at the time. But Ash thought that she had proof that she was stupid and could not possi-

1111111111111111111111111111111111111

bly lead a "normal life." She became obsessed with these thoughts and started telling everyone, including staff, that she was only eating to keep the baby alive. Her plan was to starve herself after the birth.

She was in this facility for ten days. She was released and as usual was told to follow up with her own psychiatrist and to continue with her medications. She was home a week and tried to participate in life. Her affect was flat, and a smile was a rare occurrence. She would lie in bed most of the day, only getting up to eat. She did not want to shower or talk. I sat with her daily after I got home from work and tried to encourage and support her. Nothing was getting through to her. She continued her medication but confessed that her plan was still to starve herself after the baby was born. I was still working and on edge while there. Most days, Ashton was home alone if Jim had to work. She seemed convincing when telling us that she would not kill herself until after the baby came. I had to work but was a nervous wreck while there.

One day at work, I got a call from the nurse at Ashton's mental health office. Little did I know that Ash had called the crisis hotline the previous day saying that she was suicidal and needed help. They asked her if she had an immediate plan. She told them her plan was for after the baby was born. Crisis did not feel she was in immediate danger at that time so did not go to check on her. They did however follow up the next day. They went to our home and determined that she needed to be admitted as inpatient to a facility. She was very depressed, not taking care of her personal needs, and not getting out of bed. I left work and met them all at the mental health office. Jim was already there with Ash.

CHAPTER ELEVEN

The Longest Six Weeks

An available bed was found at a hospital about forty minutes from us. Jim and I were allowed to drive Ashton to the hospital for admission. She had to go through the emergency process first before being admitted into the psychiatric unit. A crisis worker came to evaluate Ashton and, with her permission, Jim and I were allowed to stay in her room for the evaluation. They asked her if she had a suicidal plan: she detailed how she was either going to quit eating or hang herself. Boy, if that wasn't hard to sit and listen to your child state how they plan to end their life. It took all I had to hold it together at that moment. I knew of her plan to stop eating once the baby arrived, but hanging herself was new to me. The image of my daughter hanging with a rope around her neck was more than I could bear. I sat in silence with tears rolling down my face.

After the evaluation, Jim and I were permitted to escort Ash upstairs to the unit. A very compassionate nurse named Jessica took the three of us into a private room. She was so kind and proceeded to answer our millions of questions, mostly mine. I was looking for reassurance that my daughter was going to be okay. My number one question was, "Have you seen this type of behavior before and can she be treated since she is pregnant?" My other question was "Will she be safe from herself and other potentially violent patients?" Jessica explained that each case is individualized. The psychiatrist would have to find the right treatment plan, which could be difficult at this point due to the pregnancy. I so appreciated Jessica being honest with us.

She went on to inform us that the other big factor is Ashton's desire to get well. At this point, Ash had no desire to get better. Her focus was to get this pregnancy over with in order to end her own life. With this being her desire, Ash was placed with a one-to-one sitter, which helped ease my mind a bit.

Ash remained in that facility for six weeks with a one-to-one sitter due to her continued suicidal state. That was the longest six weeks for all of us.

CHAPTER TWELVE

My Faith Was Tested

As days went by, I could see my daughter getting worse. She was sinking deeper and deeper into her private hell, and I was living in mine as well. Her psychosis became like I had never seen her before. I visited every day after work, and on weekends.

There was a quiet little chapel on the entrance floor of the hospital where I would go either before or after each visit. I would sit there and either sob or beg God to help my daughter. Sometimes I would just scream out loud. I would scream out of frustration, and I felt so helpless.

I hate to admit this, but sometimes I would scream at God. I was so mad at him at times. I knew he could fix her. He was God. He had performed miracles in the past. Why wouldn't he do one now? He saw how I was suffering and how Ash was being tormented in her mind. Why wasn't he stepping in and helping us? I would tell him how I longed to have my daughter back. She was my best friend, the one I would go to whenever I needed to talk about issues, and I did not have her.

I felt so alone. He knew my heart's desire before I even asked. I really struggled with being patient. Thank goodness no one else ever came into that chapel during one of my meltdowns or I would have been committed into the psychiatric unit right alongside Ashton.

I saw Ash slipping further and further away every day. I wasn't sure how much longer she could endure this. I kept telling her to hang on, that once the baby was born the doctors could focus on treating her. I had never felt so hopeless in all my life. I should have trusted God enough to know that he was in control and had plans for Ashton's life. My faith was tested like never before, and I failed miserably. My daughter was such an amazing woman in her darkest days. Even in her severe psychotic state, she told me not to be mad at

God. She was not mad at him. Her faith never wavered.

Like I said, it was the longest six weeks.

CHAPTER THIRTEEN

The Psychosis Got Worse

Day by day, Ashton's psychosis continued to get worse. It was harder and harder for her to keep in touch with reality. Her disease took a toll on her physical appearance as well. Her face was drawn, she had bags under her eyes, and she had no desire to wash or style her long beautiful auburn hair, which she was so adamant about prior to her sickness. Although she was pregnant, she did not gain a lot of weight. She ate to provide for her unborn child only. She did not have that pregnancy glow.

Staff escorted her over to the obstetric department daily for a stress test to monitor the baby. This gave me somewhat a sense of relief to know that the baby was tolerating the stress that she was going through. Yes, the baby was a girl. Ash had found out earlier in her pregnancy that she was having a girl. Her name was Hope. I talked to Hope daily through my daughter's belly assuring her of how much her "Mawmaw" loved her. I also told her she would be fine and to hang in there.

Ashton's mental health was the worst I had ever seen it. She was hallucinating and being tortured in her mind. She slept a lot to avoid all on the conflict going on in her head. She mentioned seeing a dark figure frequently. She believed he was the devil. He would tell her to kill herself and that she wasn't worth anything. She would have vivid visual hallucinations of her younger brother being murdered. Often during our visits, she would start shaking, clench her teeth together, and then just start screaming. She told me she couldn't help it and that she felt like she was losing control. I would just hold her.

I felt so helpless. I remember cupping her face in my hands telling her to look at me. When I looked into her eyes, I saw a look of fear and terror. It was as if she was begging me with her eyes to do something and save her from her hell. I felt as though the devil was winning this battle and he wasn't going to give up until he had her soul. I knew my daughter was in there somewhere fighting the fight of her life. I kept telling her to hang on until after Hope was born, then the doctor could start her on different medications and things would get better. I even asked the doctor about taking the baby early so Ashton could start her treatment. He declined at this point stating the baby was too small and not developed enough.

Ash continued on her medication. About four weeks into her stay, the doctor decided that, due to her worsening psychosis, he had to start treating her more aggressively.   He felt comfortable that the baby was developed enough that he could safely introduce another medication. He started a second medication and explained that it would sedate the baby but felt he had no other choice. The daily trips to the obstetric department continued to monitor baby Hope.

A week into the new medication, the doctor wanted a family meeting. He was seeing no improvement in Ashton's condition and brought up the option of ECT (Electroconvulsive Therapy). He assured us that it could be safely performed during pregnancy. ECT is basically shock therapy to the brain. The doctor also explained that ECT procedures had advanced, and were not as barbaric as in the past. He also stated that it could be effective in a few treatments, but could possibly be needed throughout the patient's lifetime. The side effect would be short-term memory loss. We were not keen on the idea of having our daughter's brain messed with in that fashion, but options were running out.

Ashton had to be in agreement with the procedure, and she was not on board. Thank God!

CHAPTER FOURTEEN

Where Was God?

Speaking of God, Jim and I felt as if God had abandoned us in our deepest, darkest hour. Where was He? Why wasn't He answering our prayers? Why wasn't He helping our daughter?

Ashton told us not to be mad at God. At times, I know I doubted that He was listening. In our time of doubt, God began to speak to us through other people.

Ash told me that one day a new doctor came to see her. He asked her if she prayed. She replied that she did, but that she no longer knew what to pray for. He offered to pray with her and told her that God loves her. I told Ash that in my twenty years of nursing, I only witnessed a doctor one time who offered to pray with their patient. This does not happen often, and I believe that God was talking to her through that doctor. God was letting her know that He loved her.

Jim had an experience as well. He was at a vendor's fair that offered a Sunday morning worship service. He told me that he was standing in the crowd at that service, listening to the message and praising God. A woman approached him from behind, tapped him on the shoulder and told him that God had told her to approach him. She said that God had told her that he and his family were going through a difficult time and needed prayer. After they prayed together, the woman said, "God loves you," and walked back into the crowd.

My experience happened within a few days of Jim's and Ashton's. I had to call my Mom's hairdresser to set an appointment. I got her voice mail, which had the usual message of leave your name and number and I will return your call. The end of the message stated, "Don't forget, God loves you."

God told Jim, Ashton, and I, that He loved us through His people when we were questioning it the most. What an amazing God we serve!

One more experience that touched my heart occurred as I was driving home alone from one of our visits. I was crying as usual and feeling hopeless. To see my daughter in that state was unbearable. I would try to hold it together and be strong for Ashton during our visit. As soon as I hit my little chapel in the lobby, I would lose it. I would listen to K-Love radio station on the drive home hoping for encouragement and some sense of peace. (K-Love is a Christian radio station for those of you who are unfamiliar with it.) That particular night a beautiful song came on that I had never heard before. The title was "Praise You in This Storm" by Casting Crowns. The lyrics were so fitting at that time in my life that it seemed like a personal message from God.

Here are a few verses from that song, but I encourage you to listen to the entire song. "I was sure by now God, You would have reached down and wiped our tears away, stepped in and saved the day. But once again, I say Amen and it's still raining. As the thunder rolls, I barely hear You whisper through the rain 'I'm with you.' And as Your mercy falls, I raise my hand and praise the God who gives and takes away. I'll praise You in this storm and I will lift my hands, for You are who You are, no matter where I am. Every tear I've cried, You hold in Your hand, You never left my side. And though my heart is torn, I will praise You in this storm.[5]"

_____

[5] "Praise You In This Storm" Casting Crowns. 2005.

CHAPTER FIFTEEN

No End in Sight

Ashton's torture seemed to have no end. She remained with a one-to-one sitter. She continued to eat to provide for the baby, but still insisted that when the baby was born, she was done.

I wanted the baby to be born so that Ash could start on more medications. At the same time, I was also afraid of losing her. I did not think she would accept the medications. I also feared that she would be discharged out of the safety of the behavioral health unit and finally end her life. She was still seeing the devil and other hallucinations, but at times was lucid enough to carry on a normal conversation.

One evening during a visit, the staff asked me to meet them at the nurse's station. They showed me a full-page note that they said Ashton had written earlier in the day. Down one side of the paper was the repetitive phrase "Kill yourself, kill yourself, kill yourself," probably fifteen times. Down the other side of the paper was the same but it stated "God hates you, God hates you, God hates you." I asked the staff who wrote the note for Ash because that was not her hand writing. They assured me that she wrote it. They explained that sometimes a person's handwriting changes when they are in that state of mind. I was blown away.

Ashton's psychosis progressed to the point that the doctor decided to induce her one week early. The baby was still small, but the doctor felt that she was developed enough to be born. I took a leave of absence from work and had an attorney draw up guardianship papers for me to be Hope's temporary guardian until Ash could get well enough to come home. Ash had talked about adoption earlier but did not mention it to anyone at this facility, so the plan was for Jim and I to take Hope home after she was born. We did not know what to expect as far as Hope's health with all that she had been through. It didn't matter. She was our grandbaby and we loved her unconditionally.

CHAPTER SIXTEEN

Not One Miracle, But Two

Ashton's induction date was set for Wednesday morning.

On Sunday, she was still asking staff where she would be placed after delivering the baby because she was going to quit eating. Monday morning her mind started to clear some. Tuesday, it cleared even more. By Wednesday morning she was back to her old self and looking forward to becoming a mom.

Just like that! Some may think it was the medication. I agree that may be a part of it, but I believe that God had a big hand in it. I will never forget that day. I was overjoyed beyond words to have my daughter and best friend back. I vividly remember driving to the hospital that morning at 6:00am, marveling over the most gorgeous sunrise that God had created for our grand-daughter's arrival. I was driving and I told Jim to take the wheel. I had to capture this sunrise with my camera.

It is the cover photo on this book. It represents so much to me. The promise of a new day, the promise of a new life, the beginning of a new life for Ashton and Hope. What a privilege to be at my daughter's side to help her bring her daughter into the world. It was also a celebration of Ashton's new life that God had so graciously given her. It felt like the nightmare that we lived the past four months had finally come to and end, and we had such hope for the future.

Ashton's labor only lasted six hours after being induced. We sat through it together listening to our favorite Christian songs on my phone. Jim slept most of those six hours on the other side of the room, giving Ash and I that precious time together. When she would have a contraction, she would become silent, stare at her focal point, and when it was over would return to our conversation. Not a whimper, not a tear. I asked her, "Doesn't your contractions hurt?"

She replied, "After what I just went through in my mind, this is nothing."

When it came time to push, I was honored to be there to welcome baby Hope into our lives. When Hope was laid on Ashton's chest, the look of love was so radiant on Ashton's face. All of those horrible memories of the past months seemed to temporarily fade. She looked up at her dad and said, "Thank you so much for fighting me on the adoption."

I find Hope's name so appropriate. Shortly after Hope's birth, the rest of our family came to meet her. Gregory, Ann, and Seth brought Noel. My younger brother brought my Mom who was 95 years old at the time to meet her new great grand baby. What a perfect day. God fulfilled his promise of deliverance—deliverance of a healthy, beautiful baby girl, and deliverance of my precious daughter through her storm.

A few hours after delivery, Ash had to return to the psychiatric unit and Hope had to stay in the newborn nursery. Hope was discharged two days later. Before taking her home, Jim and I took her into our little chapel and set her in front of a big banner of Jesus. We sat and praised Him for bringing us through the fire.

We took Hope back to the hospital every day so she could bond with her Mom. The behavioral health unit made arrangements to bring Hope in a back entrance for safety reasons. We so appreciated their accommodating our daughter.

Ash was discharged five days after delivery. We had to meet with her doctor prior to discharge. I hugged him with tears in my eyes and thanked him for getting my daughter through this. He told me that it was my support that got her through. I told him that I didn't do anything, but he assured me that my daily visits had been vital to her recovery. Showing up every day and showing her how much she was loved was huge. He informed me that a lot of patients do not have that kind of support, and it makes a tremendous difference in their recovery. Honestly, there was no other place for me to be than with one of my children when they needed me.

As we were gathering up Ashton's belongings on the day of discharge, a male patient approached her and asked, "When do I get to go home?"

Ash amazed me and reminded me at that moment of the huge heart she has for others. She replied to this young man, "Do you remember the verse we talked about the other day?" and asked him to repeat it with her. It was Romans 8:18: "Wait for your joy. The pain you've been feeling can't compare to the joy that is coming." This was definitely placed in her heart by God. Ash and I had never discussed this verse before, and there she was, teaching it to others.

Ash is an amazing mother to Hope. I truly believe that Hope was sent from God to save my daughter. God knew what He was doing when he picked Ash to be Hope's mom. God has a plan for Ash's life, and this is only part of it. I admire my daughter so much for enduring such an agonizing experience and never losing her faith. Even in the midst of her suffering, she was sharing God's word with others.

CHAPTER SEVENTEEN

———————————

Unconditional Love

This is our journey: Ashton's as a person with mental illness, and mine as a mother of a child with mental illness. As the title of the book states, "Ashton's Hope; A Journey of Courage, Faith, and Unconditional Love", I believe Ash's hope in God, and in her baby, carried her through until God's healing. Courage: the courage of my daughter to fight and continue on her journey without giving up. Faith: faith that our God wants us to be happy and has plans for us far beyond our imagination. And finally, Unconditional Love, which we have witnessed first-hand. Ashton's unconditional love for Hope, our unconditional love for our daughter, and the unconditional love our God has for us.

We may be impatient with God and want things instantly, but God has a plan for each of our lives and unveils it in His time, not ours.

We have an incredible pastor at our church who I truly appreciate. He stated one Sunday, "You may have gone through something horrible that brought you to your knees to become closer with God." This trial in our life did bring us closer to God. I have learned that He knows what He is doing, and we have to be patient and trust Him.

CHAPTER EIGHTEEN

Life After the Storm

Ashton's life now if more normal than I could ever have imagined. Don't think that it is perfect, no one's life is. But at one point in my darkest days, I had my doubts about her returning to a "normal" life.

She has accepted her diagnosis of Bipolar disorder, and has learned the importance of being compliant with her treatment. Mental illness can be treated and managed. Her mental state is more stable than I have seen in fifteen years.

Baby Hope, as my other granddaughter Noel calls her, is such a joy. She is always pleasant and always smiling. I thank God daily for this little miracle that I believed saved my daughter's life. We were so worried about Hope while Ash was pregnant with her. In spite of everything that she endured before her birth, she is one happy baby. Our youngest son Seth nicknamed her "Cheeser" because she is always cheesing (smiling).

I talk with Ash just about every day. I check in with her regarding her depression and try to keep an eye out for "red flags". It is so great to have my best friend back and better than ever. I was so lost without her. She is usually the one person in this world beside by husband that I turn to when I need a shoulder to cry on. I realize that maybe down the road this horrible disease may rear it's ugly head again, but if it does I feel we are all better prepared. I know Ash has a better understanding and acceptance of her disease. She has voiced a few times that she does not wish to return to that dark place she refers to as Hell.

Ash is now engaged to a great guy who loves God. And guess what? He loves her and Hope unconditionally. God is good!

SOURCES

1. Parekh, Ranna, M.D. (n.d.) *What is Depression?* psychiatry.org. Retrieved June 08, 2020. https://www.psychiatry.org/patients-families/depression/what-is-depression

2. Mayo Clinic Staff. (n.d). *Depression (major depressive disorder).* mayoclinic.org. Retrieved June 08, 2020. https://www.mayoclinic.org/diseases-conditions/depression/symptoms-causes/syc-20356007

3. re:MIND, Depression & Bipolar Support. (n.d.). *What is Depression?* remindsupport.org. Retrieved June 08, 2020. https://www.remindsupport.org/what-is-depression/

4. Harvard Medical School. (n.d.) *What causes depression?* health.harvard.edu. Retrieved June 08, 2020. https://www.health.harvard.edu/mind-and-mood/what-causes-depression

5. Casting Crowns. (2005). Praise You In This Storm [Song]. On *Lifesong* [Album]. Beach Street/Reunion.

Made in the USA
Middletown, DE
22 September 2023

39078202R00046